HEROES FOR YOUNG READERS

GLADYS AYLWARD

Daring to Trust

Written by Renee Taft Meloche
Illustrated by Bryan Pollard

P.O. BOX 55787 SEATTLE, WA 98155

Gladys Aylward: Daring to Trust Text © 2001 by Renee Taft Meloche Illustrations © 2001 by Bryan Pollard
Published by YWAM Publishing, P.O. Box 55787, Seattle, WA 98155 ISBN 978-1-57658-228-2 Printed in China. All rights reserved.

The year was nineteen thirty.
    A woman, short and plain,
with coal black hair and dark brown eyes
    stepped on a London train.

Her name was Gladys Aylward. She
    was traveling on her own
from England to a far-off land
    called China. Old. Unknown.

She'd failed at Bible college and
    did not speak much Chinese,
but still she knew God called her there
    and so she felt at ease.

She stayed at Chinese mountain inns
    yet wasn't quite prepared
for sleeping in one long hard bed
    that everybody shared.

One morning as she looked around
       she noticed in surprise
a woman's feet all bandaged up
       and only half the size
of what two normal feet should be.
       Yet they were twice as thick.
They both were shaped like horses' hooves,
       so walking was a trick.

As Gladys watched her hobble out
       in pain that looked unbearable,
she knew it was because the Chinese
       thought big feet looked terrible.

Since men would marry women only
       if their feet were small,
the Chinese stopped the feet of girls
       from growing much at all.

Their toes were curled back underneath
       from wraps that were too tight.
This crippled them as they got old
       and made them cry at night.

Now Gladys went to Yangcheng village.
  Mountains there loomed tall.
Its roofs were shaped in cones and spheres.
  Around it stood a wall.

She learned Chinese and ran an inn
  where guests would come to know
the Bible stories Gladys told
  that happened long ago.

She told them all about God's Son
        and read from God's own Word,
and many became Christians after
        all the things they heard.

Since women's feet were bound when young,
  they were of little use,
but needing extra workers now
  to help the land produce,
the government decided feet
  no longer could be bound,
and so they asked if Gladys, who
  could easily get around,
would travel to the villages
  and go enforce the law
and take off any bindings on
  the females that she saw.

So Gladys rode by mule, then walked,
  with soldiers at her side,
to be a foot inspector through
  the rugged countryside.

She met a mother with a child
      of three upon her knee,
and said, "Unbind her bandages
      so that her feet are free."

The child's bindings were removed,
      but still her feet were white
because no blood had reached them since
      the wraps had been so tight.

So Gladys rubbed her feet 'til they
      were pink like they should be.
Her toes began to come uncurled
      and lengthen properly.

But older girls, who'd had their wraps on
      many years or more,
had feet that were too damaged now
      to grow back like before.

Eight years had passed since Gladys came
    when on a clear spring day
the Chinese heard some buzzing sounds
    that came from far away.

They rushed out of their houses. Five
    big airplanes soon appeared.
They looked like flying insects, so
    the people clapped and cheered.

As hatches opened from the planes
     and children danced about,
the Chinese saw what looked like large
     black boxes falling out.

"It's bombs!" a person shouted. "Run!"
     They heard the news and fled.
The buildings shook. Bombs hit the earth
     and total terror spread.

The buildings fell, and where they'd stood
    were gaping holes instead.
Loud cries were heard from everywhere,
    and many soon were dead.

It was the Japanese invading
    and they had a plan
to keep attacking China until
    they controlled the land.

As time went on more children lost
    their parents to the war,
so Gladys took the orphans. Soon
    they numbered ninety-four!

Since Japanese kept marching in,
    she soon thought of a plan:
she'd take the children safely to
    a town known as Sian.

With little food and shoes of cloth
        with soles of thin brown bark,
the children climbed a mountain trail
        from sunrise until dark.

The children soundly slept that night
        while Gladys stayed awake.
She thought, *With twelve more days to walk,*
        is this a big mistake?
For then we'll have to take a boat
        across the Yellow River,
then travel to Sian by train
        in hopes I can deliver
the children to an orphanage.
        She prayed a heartfelt prayer
that God would somehow make a way
        to lead them safely there.

The next day they all struggled on.
    The mountain ground was rough.
With blistered, bruised, and bloody feet
    their trip was tiring, tough.

The older girls all limped along.
    Their pain was very great
because the bindings on their feet
    had been removed too late.

So Gladys taught them hymns to sing
to keep their spirits strong.
This cheered them some, and yet they knew
the road ahead was long.

They kept on, upward, onward, with
    two older boys as guides,
when suddenly they shouted, "Soldiers!
    Hurry. We must hide."

Then Gladys stopped. She listened.
    The language was Chinese.
The soldiers who were coming toward
    them weren't their enemies!

She started to relax, but still
    she tentatively tread,
when several war planes from Japan
    came flying overhead.

They dove for cover. Looked for bombs.
    Stayed low in their ravine.
The steep and rocky landscape kept
    them all from being seen.

With shredded shoes they plodded on
    with little food to eat.
But soon they spotted something that
    put spring back in their feet.

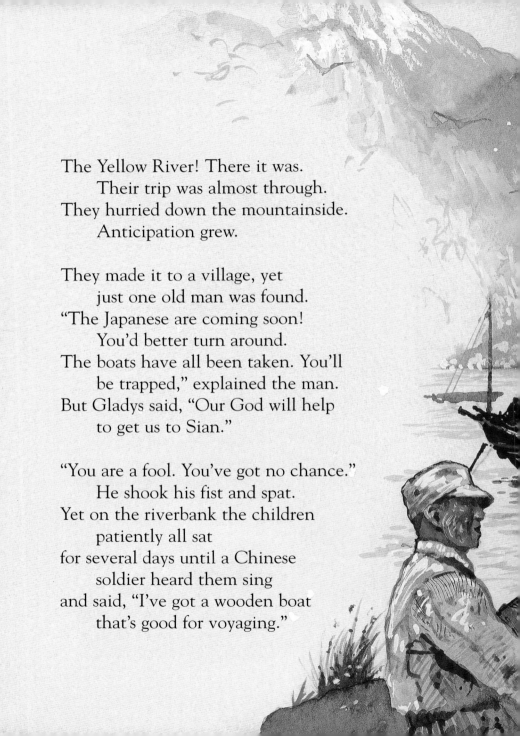

The Yellow River! There it was.
    Their trip was almost through.
They hurried down the mountainside.
    Anticipation grew.

They made it to a village, yet
    just one old man was found.
"The Japanese are coming soon!
    You'd better turn around.
The boats have all been taken. You'll
    be trapped," explained the man.
But Gladys said, "Our God will help
    to get us to Sian."

"You are a fool. You've got no chance."
    He shook his fist and spat.
Yet on the riverbank the children
    patiently all sat
for several days until a Chinese
    soldier heard them sing
and said, "I've got a wooden boat
    that's good for voyaging."

They crossed the river, took a train,
    once they'd been fully fed.
But they could not get to Sian:
    a bridge was bombed ahead.

They'd have to catch another train—
    a five-day walk from there.
They heard the news and cried out in
    exhaustion, fear, despair.

Yet God helped Gladys find the strength
    to still go on once more.
He'd take her down the path ahead
    as He had done before.

They trudged through unknown forests.
    At night they slept in caves
and listened to the howling wolves
    while trying to be brave.

They finally reached the railroad tracks
      but found to their dismay
that due to bomb threats all the routes
      were closed along the way.

Just coal trains were allowed to run.
      No passengers could travel.
The great escape that Gladys planned
      continued to unravel.

She'd have to keep her trust in God.
      She'd done her very best.
She told the children to lie down
      and try to get some rest.

She fell asleep, was woken up:
      two men were at her side.
They said the engineer decided
      all of them could ride
atop one of the big coal trains.
      What wonderful good news!
She gathered all her children round;
      there was no time to lose.

The younger ones were lifted up
    and put on several cars,
among the coals, still fast asleep,
    to slumber 'neath the stars.

Around the youngest children, older
    ones built walls of coal
so none of them would fall off when
    the train began to roll.

The next day when the children woke,
    they all shrieked with delight:
coal dust had settled over them,
    and they were black as night.

The coal dust kept them camouflaged
    from planes that might attack.
With three days left to travel, there
    was no more turning back.

But when they got to Sian, guards
    said, "Don't get off the train.
We have too many refugees.
    You simply can't remain."

Though Gladys felt like quitting and
    her energy was spent,
she knew that God would help her through
    this new predicament.

Their train continued down the track
    to Fufeng, with great speed,
and there they finally found a home.
    An orphanage agreed
to care for all the children, and
    though Gladys was worn out,
she had not lost one single child
    along the dangerous route.

Like Gladys Aylward we today
can trust God to provide
along our journey, through our lives,
to be our faithful guide.

Christian Heroes: Then & Now

by Janet and Geoff Benge

Heroes for Young Readers and Heroes of History for Young Readers are based on the Christian Heroes: Then & Now and Heroes of History biographies by Janet and Geoff Benge. Don't miss out on these exciting, true adventures for ages ten and up!

Continued on the next page...

Heroes of History

by Janet and Geoff Benge

Abraham Lincoln: A New Birth of Freedom
Alan Shepard: Higher and Faster
Benjamin Franklin: Live Wire
Christopher Columbus: Across the Ocean Sea
Clara Barton: Courage under Fire
Daniel Boone: Frontiersman
Douglas MacArthur: What Greater Honor
George Washington Carver: From Slave to Scientist
George Washington: True Patriot
Harriet Tubman: Freedombound
John Adams: Independence Forever
John Smith: A Foothold in the New World
Laura Ingalls Wilder: A Storybook Life
Meriwether Lewis: Off the Edge of the Map
Orville Wright: The Flyer
Theodore Roosevelt: An American Original
Thomas Edison: Inspiration and Hard Work
William Penn: Liberty and Justice for All

...and more coming soon. Unit Study Curriculum Guides are also available.

Heroes for Young Readers Activity Guides
Educational and Character-Building Lessons for Children

by Renee Taft Meloche

Heroes for Young Readers Activity Guide for Books 1–4
Gladys Aylward, Eric Liddell, Nate Saint, George Müller

Heroes for Young Readers Activity Guide for Books 5–8
Amy Carmichael, Corrie ten Boom, Mary Slessor, William Carey

Heroes for Young Readers Activity Guide for Books 9–12
Betty Greene, David Livingstone, Adoniram Judson, Hudson Taylor

Heroes for Young Readers Activity Guide for Books 13–16
Jim Elliot, Cameron Townsend, Jonathan Goforth, Lottie Moon
Heroes of History for Young Readers Activity Guide for Books 1–4
George Washington Carver, Meriwether Lewis, George Washington, Clara Barton

...and more coming soon.

Designed to accompany the vibrant Heroes for Young Readers books, these fun-filled Activity Guides lead young children through a variety of character-building and educational activities. Pick and choose from the activities or follow the included thirteen-week syllabus. An audio CD with book readings, songs, and fun activity tracks is available for each Activity Guide.

For a free catalog of books and materials contact
YWAM Publishing, P.O. Box 55787, Seattle, WA 98155
1-800-922-2143 www.ywampublishing.com